S

I Attempted 🦋 She Committed

by: Sara Deno

Suicide is a
Permanent Solution
to a Temporary Problem
Choose Life!

Published by ENA Center
Escanaba, Michigan

© 2020 ENA Center

ISBN: 978-1-7360225-0-4

Library of Congress Control Number:
2020949110

First Edition 2020

10   9   8   7   6   5   4   3   2   1

Published by ENA Center
Escanaba, Michigan

Dedication

This book is dedicated to my mom who loves me unconditionally, my husband who is my strength and my happy place, my boys who give me reasons to live, and my sister Ena who inspires me to save others when I was unable to save her.

Ena
May 27, 1981 – March 14, 2016

The World is
Better with
YOU in it!

Introduction:

Not everyone understands how it feels to have depression and thoughts of suicide. A friend of mine in college would say, "You just have to choose to be positive." I always wished it could be that simple. For some, I think it is. I believe their brain is wired differently, which is why they can't comprehend depression and suicide. But for me and many others, I think it is in our DNA. I think we are born with these negative thoughts and feelings. So not everyone may understand, but many do. You are not alone! I think our brains can be rewired through hard work and support. Don't be ashamed to ask for help. Let me tell you my story in hopes it helps you Choose Life.

Go with the
Flow

Part 1:

In the summer of 1999, I attempted suicide.

I had just completed my second year at college. The first two years, I lived at my grandma's cousin's house. She charged me $5 per day for the days I stayed there. The most I paid was $25 per week because I went home on the weekends. I could afford that. I would work during the summer to save money to pay my rent. That way, I didn't have to work while going to college. Getting good grades was always very important to me. I was a perfectionist and wasn't happy with anything less than an A. I couldn't live at the same place in the fall. Grandma's cousin was selling her house. I would need to find a new place to live.

In anticipation of housing being much higher, I got two jobs that summer. It was my third summer working at the chiropractic office. I had decided in 10th grade that I was going to be a chiropractor. I had volunteered at the office my senior year in high school as part of my Health Occupations class. They hired me on as a receptionist for the summers. I didn't feel like I was getting enough hours at

The sky is the limit.

the chiropractic office to save money. I applied at the casino and got a job as a Keno runner. My boss in Keno was great. She worked around my other schedule. I worked days at the office and nights and weekends at the casino. I loved both jobs, but it was stressful.

Dr. Mary, my boss at the chiropractic office, was my idol. I put her so high on a pedestal that I would never even come close to being as great as her. I wanted to please her so much. When she asked me to clean the office on the weekends, I said yes. When she asked me to cut the grass, I said yes. When she asked me to work on a computer project, I said yes. The whole time I was still working at Keno. The stress was getting overwhelming. I asked my mom to help me by cleaning the office while I cut the grass. It was still a chore as I had to bring my own lawn mower. I started to wear out and get tired. One day, I made a mistake. I can't even remember what I did. But, I remember Dr. Mary yelling at me for it. Well, she probably didn't actually yell, but I felt like I had been chewed up and spit out. I didn't want to disappoint her or get in trouble again. But, the harder I tried, the more mistakes I made.

Reflection turns a mistake into a lesson

Keno was the opposite. It was relaxing and fun. I would walk around the casino yelling "Keno" and talking to people. I sold Keno tickets and got to know many of the regulars. I also knew most of the floor workers: slot attendants, security, cashiers, and maintenance. I kept a big smile on my face. The hours I worked Keno were like an escape from reality. No disappointed idol, no money worries, and no care about home life. So, I worked as many hours as I could.

Home life was changing. Normally, I lived at my mom's house. This summer, my brother and I were not getting along. He would have friends over at late hours. It was sometimes hard to sleep with their music. He would try to boss me around. I would tell him off. I wanted to get my own place but didn't think I could afford it. Then, I met Dan at the casino. I started hanging out with him and found out he needed a new place to live too. Dan and I decided to get an apartment together. I only had one real relationship before meeting Dan. In my mind, he and I were a couple moving in together. Was I wrong! The very first night in our apartment, he brought home a girl. I had meant nothing

Give Yourself a Break.

Everyone needs one once in a while.

to him. Over the four weeks or so that we lived together, he must have had a girl, a friend, or a group of friends at the apartment almost every day. Our walls were paper thin and it was even harder to sleep than with my brother's music. I wanted to move out, but I had signed a lease.

My mind was so full of thoughts and worries all the time. I was working 60-80 hours a week between the two jobs. Instead of saving money for college in the fall, I was blowing it on an apartment. The apartment was worse than my mom's house. I had to come home to a guy I use to like and listen to him having fun with his new girlfriend or laughing with his friends. I was over worked, over tired, and over stressed. I kept making mistakes and disappointing people and/or myself. My soul was in pain. It felt like my heart and soul were being crushed and suffocated. It hurt so bad inside, my only temporary escape was Keno. I would smile and pretend life was great. Most of the time, it was like wearing a mask to fool others. Once in a while, I would fool myself for a few moments.

We don't go in circles...

We spiral

I was struggling and I knew it. I talked to my doctor who prescribed Effexor, an antidepressant. I think I had only been on Effexor for a week. I didn't realize it was making things worse. It was making it easier to wear the mask and be very happy for others. But, it was also making the pain inside worse. Being alone was hard and I felt like I had no one to talk to. Every day was a struggle. The little failures kept piling up and up. Finally, the last straw broke and I attempted suicide.

That day, I worked at the chiropractic office during the day. I remember my coworker telling me to get a good night's sleep. The boss had asked her if I was tired lately. After my shift there, I went straight to the casino to work my Keno shift. I told Dan not to have people over because I needed to sleep. But after work, I went home to find Dan and his girlfriend. I went to bed but couldn't sleep. They were watching TV and laughing. The walls were thin and they were sitting right against my bedroom wall. I snapped. I couldn't do anything right. I couldn't make anyone happy. I didn't belong anywhere. I couldn't even sleep. I yelled at Dan and they left. But, it was too late. I couldn't do it

Stand Tall. Don't let anyone knock you down.

anymore. The pain was too intense. My soul was being crushed and I was suffocating. I was sick of fighting to get through each day. I wanted to go back to when I was happy and carefree. I wanted to be with my Grandpa who had died when I was six. I went to the bathroom and collected all the pills from our medicine cabinet. I went to the kitchen and found a ½ bottle of wine. I sat in the living room crying my eyes out, listening to music, and washing down the pills. I was going to be at peace with my Papa. Everyone would be better without me. I wouldn't be a disappointment to anyone. I wouldn't fail and let them down. They wouldn't have to worry about me. Their lives would be better without me. I swallowed the last pill I had.

Instantly, I regretted my decision. I didn't really want to die; I just didn't want to hurt anymore. But now, my mom would hurt. My mind went to her and I knew that she loved me. I couldn't die. I wanted to live.

I called my best friend at 3:00 am in the morning. I told her what I did and that she needed to come make me puke. She came. She left her husband and baby to come save me. The moment she walked in the door, I ran

It's ok to fall...

Just keep getting up.

to the bathroom and started to vomit. I don't know how long my head was in the toilet. I remember Dan and his girlfriend coming back. He said he would take care of me, so my best friend left. I remember Dan yelling at me. He said what I did was selfish. I hadn't thought of it that way at the time. Now, I felt guilty. Eventually, I moved from the toilet to my bed. I continued to vomit in my garbage can. I was supposed to work at the chiropractic office. Dan called and told them I was sick.

I can't remember how many days I called in sick to my jobs. I remember hanging my head off the bed into the garbage can. I vomited off and on for three days. At first, the vomit was shades of yellow to green. After a while, it turned black and looked like coffee grounds (Later, I learned that coffee ground vomit is from partially digested blood. My stomach or esophagus was bleeding). I was afraid I would never stop vomiting. I finally called my mom. I told her what I did and asked her to take me to the hospital. I asked her not to tell anyone because I was embarrassed of my attempt. At the ER, they gave me meds to stop the vomiting. They pumped me with fluids for dehydration. I had

Cherish your friends. Good ones are hard to find.

to talk to a counselor before I could be discharged. The counselor had to make sure I wasn't going to attempt suicide again if I left. Eventually, I got to go home. I was going to live. I promised my mom that I would never attempt again (and I haven't).

The pain wasn't over. My esophagus hurt. I couldn't drink anything without pain for a whole week. It hurt to eat anything for three weeks. But, the esophagus pain deadened the internal pain. I realized the antidepressant had made things worse. I was afraid to try them again. I still needed help. I was still wearing a mask. When I returned to work at Keno, one of the guys I worked with told me something I will never forget. He said that I was his hero because I was always smiling. I didn't have the heart to tell him it was just a mask; I had just tried to commit suicide the week before. I wished I was as happy as I looked. I decided to try counseling. My whole life I believed asking for help was a sign of weakness. It is not! Asking for help is a sign of strength.

Since my suicide attempt, I have had many ups and downs in life. I have learned to ask for help. With the help and close monitoring of a doctor and a counselor, who worked

with me, I found an anti-anxiety/anti-depressant medication that works for me. I have learned that rewiring the brain toward the positive requires daily positive input. I read a lot of self-help books. When not in counseling, I have friends I talk to. Journaling and getting the thoughts out is freeing. Sometimes, the best I can do is just get through the day. When I can't find the self-love to help myself, helping others makes me feel better. And, one of my favorite things to do now is something I learned from the book *How to Stop Worrying and Start Living* by Dale Carnegie. I think of "the worst thing that can happen." Then, I think of ways to deal with it instead of just worrying. But, I always remember I am not alone. I ask for help before the final straw breaks.

These techniques have worked for me. I am married to my best friend. I actually met him in 1999 shortly after my suicide attempt. We were friends for six years before I truly realized that he is the best man I have ever known. We have two amazing boys. I own my own chiropractic business. Being the owner is challenging but gives me flexibility to do the things that are most important. To me, family,

Leave Footprints

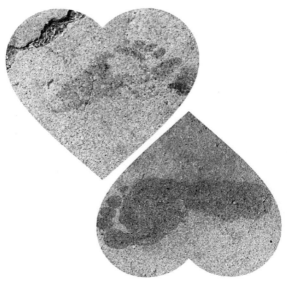

In the Hearts of Others

friends, and the other people in our lives are the most important thing in life.

You are part of my "other people." When I look at the world, I see how we are all different. We are all equal in that we are human beings. But, we are all different. To me, different isn't bad; it is good! It is what makes us special. We are all unique and special in our own way. We all have a purpose and a niche. Sometimes, we just need help finding our place in this world. That is why I am telling you my story. Not because I like to talk about it, but because you might relate to a part of it. You might see similarities in your current struggle. You might realize You are not alone! You are special and important! Choose life and ask for help because there is something better waiting for you. You just have to move forward and you will find your purpose and your niche. The world has a special place for you and will not be better off without you! You will eventually get there. The only way you will ever truly fail is if you give up and commit suicide. So, ask for help! Choose Life!

Have Faith!

Life can turn out better than your wildest dreams.

Part 2:

I will never forget the day my sister committed suicide.

She called me before work and asked me to cosign a loan for $3000. She said she wanted to go to a biker's rally because all of her friends from California were going to be there. She said that it may be the last time she could see them. She hadn't seen any of them since she moved back to Michigan eight years earlier.

I could hear the pleading in her voice as she asked. I was so mad at her for putting me in that pickle. I wanted to help her. But, she didn't have the best track record with repaying loans. I couldn't afford to pay the loan. And, I definitely couldn't afford to have my credit wrecked. I figured my husband would be pissed off if I said yes without talking to him first.

I told her no. She begged me to help. She offered to drop the loan to $2000. She said the payments were only $50/month and she could afford that. She asked me to please think about it. I told her I would think about it because I couldn't stand the pleading in her voice.

Everything and
Everyone has a
Purpose,
even if we don't
know what it is.

As the day went on, I continued to be mad. How could she put me between a rock and a hard place like this? I couldn't afford to take a vacation, but I was supposed to help her go on one. She didn't have a real job. She got paid maybe $300/month for helping take care of my mom who has major depression. How was she going to pay the loan with that little to live on? I couldn't stand to hear her disappointment. I texted her and told her I couldn't help. I felt bad.

I had a busy day at work and now I had to deal with all this stress on top of it. I called my brother on my lunch break to vent. She had called and asked him for help too. He had told her one of the same things, "save money and then go." Then, he told me something else. He said he thought she was going to try to kill herself. I got soooo mad. She had attempted suicide at least three times in the past that I knew of. Each time, she had taken pills. Each time, she had been found, rushed to the hospital, had her stomach pumped and was saved. I felt like she was crying wolf to get what she wanted. My anger blurted out, "Well if she is going to kill herself, then she will just have to kill herself. We can't just give

Never let the fear
of striking out
keep you from
playing the game.
-Babe Ruth

her money every time she threatens to." I didn't mean it. I was just so mad at her. Or maybe, I was mad at myself for not being able to afford to help her.

I finished with my work day and went home. I told my husband about the request for money. He said we could help if she got at least a part-time job. I told him I was going to talk to her because my brother was worried she would kill herself. I grabbed my phone and as I headed to the car I received a text.

"Grama's truck is parked at the bottom of Sugarloaf. The keys are above the visor. I am going to a better place."

Instant panic set in. I didn't mean what I said. I didn't want her to die. She can't die thinking I don't care. I care. I love her. She is my little sister. I should protect her. I have to save her.

I tried calling her to talk her out of it. She didn't answer. I ran and got my husband's phone. The battery was going dead on mine so I plugged it in. I was stuck at the kitchen cupboard. On one phone, I kept calling my sister, letting it ring until the voicemail picked up, hanging up, and dialing again. On the other phone, I called my mom to see if the text

GO THROUGH THE DARKNESS

TO FIND THE LIGHT AT THE END OF THE TUNNEL.

could be real. I didn't tell my mom about the text. I just asked where my sister was. She said she had left with my Grama's truck about 1 ½ hours ago. That made the text possible. I called 911 and asked to be transferred to Marquette dispatch. I told them my sister was at Sugarloaf to commit suicide and to send someone to save her. I kept calling her and she still wouldn't answer. I decided to text. Maybe, she would read it. I texted, "don't' do it!" Then, "I love you!" I figured the police should be there by then, so I quit calling. I called the Marquette dispatch for an update. They told me they found her but didn't have any more information.

A small ray of hope shimmered on what I feared the reality would be. Maybe they found her in time. Maybe they were too busy to call me because they were rushing her to the ER to get her stomach pumped. Maybe she would be ok like the other three times she tried to commit suicide by taking pills. But, I couldn't sit there and wait. I had to do damage control.

First, I went to talk to my brother. I had to let him know what was going on. I told him I was going to see mom on my way home. My mom had problems with major depression.

The only impossible
journey is the one
you never begin.
-Tony Robbins

We feared this would push her over the edge. We would have to have her hospitalized. I called my brother-in-law, who worked for dispatch, and asked him what would happen if my sister died. He said they would send police to my mom's house to notify her. I asked him to make sure that NO one contacted my mom. He said he would make sure they contacted me. Next, I came up with a perfectly good lie to tell my mom. I went to her house and lied, "Ena wanted me to tell you that she is staying with a friend in Marquette tonight. She couldn't call you because the battery on her phone was going dead." My mom replied, "Then why is she at the hospital?" WTF??!! My mom had called my sister's phone repeatedly and eventually someone at the hospital answered and told her my sister was there. That is all they would tell her. They messed up my perfectly good lie. So, I told her about the text and not to worry. I told her Ena was probably fine if she was at the hospital. She probably had her stomach pumped. She probably didn't want to talk to anyone. She hadn't wanted to talk to anyone the last time she had been hospitalized for a

HANG ON

DON'T LEAVE

suicide attempt. With all these probabilities, I got my mom calmed down and headed home.

When I turned the corner onto my street, I saw the police car in front of my house. I knew what I had known deep down all night. She was dead. I think that is why I didn't jump in my car and head to Marquette the moment I got the text. Deep inside, I knew there was nothing I could do to save her and I couldn't bear to be present for the outcome. Walking up to the police officer, I said, "my sister's dead, isn't she?" Surprisingly, the response was "we are waiting for confirmation." Why the hell would they come to my house if it wasn't already confirmed? Moments later, which seemed like an awkward 5-10 minutes, he declared she was dead. He gave me a phone number for the officer in Marquette who could give me more information, told me we could call victim services for help, and left. That is all I remember.

I don't remember if I called the Marquette officer right away or not. When I talked to him, he told me that on his way up Sugarloaf Mountain he heard the single gunshot. He said he got to her as quick as possible and tried to help but it was too late. She died almost

Love Like A Dog...

Unconditionally!

immediately. I imagined what he had to see. I felt bad for him as he told me he tried to help. He sounded devastated that he didn't get to her sooner. What he saw and how he felt must have been horrible. I didn't want him to remember her like that. I told him to dispose of the gun because I didn't want to see it. I didn't want to remember her like that either. I sent him a letter with a memorial card a week later. I have never heard from him again, but I think of him often and hope he is well. I also can't remember if I cried that night. I know I was busy taking care of everyone, but I don't remember how I reacted. I just remember being kind of detached from my reality.

I went to my brother's first and told him and his family. He felt like it might be his fault because of things he had said while also denying her the loan. I told him it wasn't. But, I thought to myself that I could use that on my mom. We had to go tell my mom and I feared a nervous breakdown. I thought if I could give her something else to think about maybe she would be ok. My brother and I went to tell my mom. She burst into tears. I couldn't imagine the pain of losing a child. I lost a sister, but losing a child must be unbearable. I hugged

You'll never know how far you can reach until you try.

her and told her, "Mom, you have to pull it together for us." I told her she had to be strong for my brother because he felt like it was his fault. She had always done things to take care of my brother and I thought she might pull herself through if she kept her mind on him instead of herself. I left my brother with my mom and walked next door to tell my grandma. When I went back to check on my mom, she had calmed down enough and told us we could go home. I told her I would call her after checking my work schedule so we could go make arrangements.

The next day, life went forward even though I wanted it to pause. I woke up, got ready for work, got my kids ready, dropped them off at school, and went to work. I had a large gap between clients, so I called my mom and told her we would make arrangements then.

Shortly after but thankfully awhile before my first client, I got a call from the hospital. Of all the things I had to do when my sister died, this for some reason hit me the hardest. They wanted to know if we wanted to donate her organs. They said her skin was still usable. I couldn't remember what she had wanted. I thought that legally, it would be my mother's

Some days you just have to say...

Dam It!

decision because she was the closer living relative. I forgot all about the Power of Attorney my sister had given me three years prior. I feared asking my mom would put her over the edge and she would be headed to the psych ward for sure. I explained this to the lady and said as much as I wanted to help other people, I couldn't. She was very kind. She said that I was helping because I was helping my mother. When I hung up the phone, I literally hit the floor. I melted into a puddle and sobbed hysterically. I don't know how long I laid there. It felt like forever. I was glad no one was there to see me. Eventually, I ran out of tears, composed myself, and put on my mask. My happy face could cover the deepest pain imaginable. I just had to shove all those feelings away for a little bit.

Between clients, we went to the funeral home to make arrangements. We didn't have a lot of money to put on a big to-do. I wanted something really nice. My sister wanted to be cremated, but we had to see her. We scheduled a private viewing followed by cremation. A tiny obituary was written to publish in the local paper. It basically said she died and was survived by her parents. We picked out an urn

You miss 100%
of the shots you
don't take.
-Wayne Gretzky

and memorial cards. I wrote a mini eulogy for the back of her memorial card. Picking a stock poem seemed so impersonal. We decided to have a Celebration of Life instead of a funeral. I would host it at my office so we didn't have to pay to use the funeral home. The kind funeral director let me borrow picture boards.

After leaving the funeral home, we ran to DHS to apply for funeral funds and made a few notification calls. Calling to tell people was hard. But, I had to do it. I remember calling my two best friends while driving to work the next day. I was alone in the car and I could cry. I have always felt like it is only ok to cry in private. When I can't control the tears and they fall in front of others, I feel so embarrassed. So, I called my best friends in the car by myself. I cried. There are still many days I cry in the car by myself. It is ok to cry! I have a hard time holding the tears in now as I write this.

My two best friends and my husband took care of me while I took care of everyone else. One of my friends took off work and traveled to come for the memorial. She helped me sort through all of my pictures to find ones of my sister for the boards. Both of my friends and

Small pebbles can make big ripples.

their moms came to the memorial. The four of them ran the kitchen for me. They took care of "the little things" so that I could focus on talking to everyone who came. My husband stood by me and gave me the strength to get through each day and task. Just being there to help me was the kindest gift I could have ever received. To know I had them to take care of me was priceless.

I had to take care of extra people the day of my sister's viewing. The viewing was for immediate family only. My uncle, his wife, and a neighbor showed up because wires got crossed. They thought it was for everyone. As politely as I could, I asked them to leave. My mom, grandma, brother, sister-in-law, husband, and myself were the only ones that got to see my sister. It was hard. We all gathered around her as she lay on a table. Her bottom half was covered by a sheet. She was wearing one of her favorite shirts that we had brought. Her arms lay over the sheet so we could hold her hands. She looked like she was sleeping and I so wished she could wake up. It felt like we stood with her forever but only a few minutes at the same time. I told the funeral director to send her favorite shirt with

WHEN YOU GIVE A HUG...

YOU GET A HUG

her and to also burn the clothes she had been wearing when she died. We got her purse and jewelry, but I couldn't bear the thought of seeing her clothes.

After the viewing, my brother, sister-in-law, husband, and I went to Hudson's restaurant. We sat at the bar drinking cranberry and vodka (one of my sister's favorite drinks) and telling stories about her. My sister was a story teller and I always felt like she embellished and made up a lot of things. But that day, I found out she didn't exaggerate as much as I thought. I felt like the son in the movie "Big Fish" and my sister was the dad. Her far-fetched stories were true. One story was that she tackled the lead singer of Godsmack while working security at Rock USA. I always thought she was making it up. I thought she went to Rock USA and just told us she was working. And if she really tackled him, it would be all over Facebook. But, I was wrong. My brother confirmed that his friend saw her tackle the guy from Godsmack. He had taken one of the security golf carts and she got it back. I also found an email on her computer from the head of security asking her if she would be coming back that year. I pictured it

Every Day is a New Beginning

in my head and I laughed. It felt good to laugh thinking about her. I loved to tell stories and remember her having fun. It made me feel closer to her. It also made me miss her and feel sad. But, I wanted to remember her good life and not just her bad ending. I wanted others to remember her that way too.

For her Celebration of Life, I set up tables and chairs in one room of my office. A picnic table was put in another. Food was spread out in the kitchen. In the main room, I set up a table with the urn and a couple flowers we picked out for her. A purple iris was what I bought. Her favorite color was purple. Picture boards were set up in convenient spots. The idea was to eat and share fond memories. When the main room was full, I gave a eulogy. I had written a few pages to read to make up for the short obituary. With the help of God and my husband by my side, I was able to read every word clearly without bursting into tears. The rest of the time I buzzed back and forth talking to people, checking on my kids, and making sure no one broke the barrier I set up to block my recep-tionist's desk. I can remember parts of the day

YOUR LIFE IS WORTH MORE THAN THE WORDS ON A HEADSTONE.

clearly as if they just happened. Other parts are a blur. It was a nice Celebration of Life.

Life kept going for the rest of us after that day. It isn't better without her. It is hard. I miss her. I have mixed emotions: sadness, hope, guilt, shock, disbelief, anger, regret, failure, extreme loss, numbness, pain, and acceptance. Sometimes they are all in the same day. These feelings never go away. Some days are better than others. Nothing will ever bring her back. I will never quit missing her. Part of me will always feel guilty for not saving her. I will always be sad that she is missing important things in our life. I will always imagine "What if she was still here?" When I remember the good times with her, I feel blessed to have had her in my life. I know her life mattered. I just wish she would have known she was important. I wish she had stayed to find her niche. I wish she could have known how much this tragedy would change our lives for the worse. I wish I could yell at her when I get mad at her and tell her how stupid her decision was. I wish she had known how much pain her decision would cause and will continue to cause forever. I wish I could yell at her for leaving me. I wish I could play

Don't wait for the storm to pass...

Play in the rain!

Mexican Train Dominoes with her. I wish I could laugh with her. I wish I could hug her and tell her how much I love her. I wish...

My wish for you, as you read this, is to realize that someone in your life feels this way about you. Someone in your life will have to go through these painful events. You might not think that anyone feels this way. But, I guarantee if you commit suicide, it will change their life for the worse. It will change the world for the worse. You are important and special! Your life has a purpose! You will be missed deeply! Please be strong and ask for help. Remember, You are not alone! Sometimes people are too busy with their own lives to notice you need help. So, ask! There is someone who would love to help you. If you can't think of anyone, call the National Suicide Prevention Lifeline at 1-800-273-8255 or go on their website at: suicidepreventionlifeline.org to start a chat. They want to help you. I want to help you. This book was written with the sole purpose of helping you. Suicide is a Permanent Solution to a Temporary Problem. Please Choose Life!

It's easier for people to love you if...

You Come Out of Your Shell.

After Thoughts

Before sharing my story with strangers, I had to run it past trusted family and friends. I still seek the approval of others even in my forties. I had two people who gave interesting responses that I would like to share.

My mom noted that my brother, she, and I all felt like we were responsible for my sister's suicide. Not that she committed suicide because of us, but that we didn't see the signs and stop her. She pondered, "I wonder if everyone feels responsible?"

My trusted friend then noted that she cried after reading about my suicide attempt. She said, "I can't believe I saw you every single day and had no idea you were feeling that way." I told her that I didn't let anyone see. I didn't want anyone to think badly of me as I already thought badly of myself.

You never know what people are going through on the inside. So, just BE KIND!

Be the
Character

You were
meant to Be

Resources I recommend
that have helped me:

1) Anything by Sam Glenn
   a. The video of his story about falling off an airplane is hilarious.
   b. *Butt Prints in the Sand (Simple Ways of Doing Something Great with Your Life)*
   c. *Who Put a Lizard in My Lasagna? – Using the Best of Who You Are to Create the Best of What You Want*
   d. Countless other books or videos

2) *How to Stop Worrying and Start Living* by Dale Carnegie

3) *You Are a Badass: How to Stop Doubting Your Greatness and Start Living an Awesome Life* by Jen Sincero

4) Any Mars and Venus book by John Gray, I've read:
   a. *Men Are From Mars, Women Are From Venus*
   b. *Mars And Venus On A Date*
   c. *Mars And Venus Together Forever*

5) Rachel Hollis' books
   a. *Girl, Wash Your Face: Stop Believing the Lies About Who You Are so You Can Become Who You Were Meant to Be*

Believe in
Miracles
Angels are
Among Us

b. *Girl, Stop Apologizing: A Shame-Free Plan for Embracing and Achieving Your Goals*

6) *You Can Heal Your Life* by Louise Hay

7) Currently reading: *Best Self: Be You, Only Better* by Mike Bayer

8) www.butterflyinsight.com/purple-butterfly-color-meaning-and-myths.html

   a. To me, the butterfly represents change. Some people say that butterflies are from Heaven. Purple was my sister's favorite color. A beautiful purple butterfly painting by Sam Glenn was my inspiration for the cover of the book.

   b. After creating the book cover, I googled the meaning of the purple butterfly out of curiosity. The website: butterflyinsight.com came up on the top of the list. It is some really interesting reading. The one sentence that really seemed fitting for this book was "If one has been feeling sad or under the weather, a purple butterfly can indicate that healing will soon take place." May this book help you on your journey to heal.

**National Suicide Prevention
Lifeline call: 1-800-273-8255
Or chat at: suicidepreventionlifeline.org**

IF YOU ARE ALWAYS LOOKING

IN THE PAST...

YOU MAY MISS WHAT IS IN FRONT OF YOU!

ENA CENTER

Eliminating Negative Attitudes

ENA Center was created to help people by providing access to light therapy, self-help materials, and relaxation at an affordable price.

When my sister Ena passed away, I was having a hard time and tried to get counseling to help me through. I was unable to schedule an appointment in a timely manner. So, I started reading self-help books and listening to audio tapes. It made a big change in my attitude. Instead of continuing to be sad, I decided to turn a horrible loss into a positive tribute. It is because of my journey that I decided to open ENA Center to help other people Eliminate Negative Attitudes.

My vision for the future of ENA Center is for it to be booked year round. We will have to open more rooms to accommodate all the appointments. People will soak up light in the winter and take personal relaxation time for themselves in the summer. Someday it will be a non-profit organization with ENA Centers all over the US.

About The Author

Sara Deno has completed both Applied Suicide Intervention Skills Training (ASIST) and SafeTalk training through LivingWorks. Passionate about helping people, she wears many hats on a daily basis as a wife, mother, Doctor of Chiropractic, bookkeeper, caregiver, business owner, author, and founder of ENA Center: Eliminating Negative Attitudes.